The Simple Abundance

Journal of Gratitude

Sarah Ban Breathnach

GRAND CENTRAL
PUBLISHING

NEW YORK   BOSTON

Grand Central Publishing
Hachette Book Group
1290 Avenue of the Americas, New York, NY 10104
grandcentralpublishing.com
twitter.com/grandcentralpub

Originally published in paper over board by Grand Central Publishing
in November 1996
Revised Edition: December 2019

Grand Central Publishing is a division of Hachette Book Group, Inc. The Grand
Central Publishing name and logo is a trademark of Hachette Book Group, Inc.

The publisher is not responsible for websites (or their content) that are not owned
by the publisher.

The Hachette Speakers Bureau provides a wide range of authors for speaking events.
To find out more, go to www.hachettespeakersbureau.com or call (866) 376-6591.

ISBN: 978-1-5387-3508-4 (paper over board)

Printed in the United States of America

LSC-C

10 9 8 7 6 5 4 3 2 1

IF THE ONLY PRAYER
YOU EVER SAY
IN YOUR ENTIRE LIFE
IS THANK YOU,
IT WILL BE ENOUGH.

—Meister Eckhart

For Oprah
with love
THANK YOU.

Simple Abundance

In daily life, we must see that it is not happiness that makes us grateful. It is gratefulness that makes us happy.

—Brother David Steindl-Rast

There is a wonderful Hasidic parable about the power of gratitude to change the course of our destiny in a heartbeat, the speed I imagine it takes for a "thank you" to reach Heaven's ears.

Once upon a time, when times were tough, two men—both poor farmers—were walking down a country lane and met their Rabbi. "How is it for you?" the Rabbi asked the first man.

"Lousy," he grumbled, bemoaning his lot and lack. "Terrible, hard, awful. Not worth getting out of bed for. Life is lousy."

Now, God was eavesdropping on this conversation. "Lousy?" the Almighty thought. "You think your life is lousy now? I'll show you what lousy is, you ungrateful lout."

Then the Rabbi turned to the second man. "And you, my friend?"

"Ah, Rabbi—life is good. God is so gracious, so generous. Each morning when I awaken, I'm so grateful for the gift of another day, for I know, rain or shine, it will unfold in wonder and blessings too bountiful to count. Life is so good."

God smiled as the second man's thanksgiving soared upwards until it became one in harmony with the heavenly hosts. Then the Almighty roared with delighted laughter. "Good? You think your life is good now? I'll show you what *good* is!"

Just the thought of the blessings this fortunate farmer was about to receive makes me smile. By giving thanks, the blessed farmer set in motion the spiritual law embodied in the phrase, "As above, so below." For every action in the Universe, there is an equal reaction. That reaction can be complementary to the original action or its absolute opposite, as we saw in the attitudes of the two farmers. As the seventeenth-century English poet John Milton tells us: "Good, the more Communicated, more abundant grows."

The Grace of Gratitude

Grace fills empty spaces, but it can only enter where there is a void to receive it, and it is grace itself which makes this void.

—Simone Weil

Gratitude is the most passionate transformative force in the Cosmos. When we offer thanks to God or to another human being, Gratitude gifts us with renewal, reflection, and reconnection. Gratitude bestows reverence, allowing us to encounter and embrace everyday epiphanies, those transcendent moments of awe that change forever how we perceive the world and experience Life. Is it abundant or is it poor?

Do you feel as if your glass is half full today or is it half empty?

Often, it's difficult to know exactly how we feel because we exist in a relentless flood of breaking news, where our senses are continually assaulted, our self-esteem is plundered, and truth/trust has become the first casualty of the social media wars. Unable to identify the source of our distress, we feel fraught, frightened, fragile—fractured in every part of our daily round. Grappling during these days of doubt and nights of sad brooding has worn us down to a raveling, and we barely know how to recognize, express, or repair it. But Gratitude does.

For many of us, our psychic early warning systems have been set on the default position of "High Alert" for much too long. This keeps us on guard for any lurking danger—real, imagined, or invisible.

All too often, it's the imaginary scenarios that scare us the most. That's because our three most precious natural resources—time, creative energy, and emotion—are strip-mined daily by technology. We find our souls unprotected as the cornerstones of our spiritual birthright—faith, optimism, courage, honor, and hope—erode and become unwilling victims of the guerilla war for our attention. When there is no imagination or inspiration, ignorance and intimidation rush in to take their place.

The nineteenth-century American philosopher and "father of American psychology," William James, described our contemporary dilemma over a century ago in this way: "The world is full of partial stories that run parallel to one another, beginning and ending at odd times. They mutually interlace and interfere at points, but we cannot unify them completely in our minds."

So, with great gusto, we do the next best thing to try to create a unified, healthy—maybe even sacred—life for ourselves: We grow our own organic vegetables or pay others to provide them. We're sure to take our vitamins, drink filtered water, sip protein and probiotic shakes, join book clubs or Facebook groups. We stretch with yoga, sweat on high-intensity bicycles, and then treat ourselves with low-fat rice sorbet.

And you wonder why we're perpetually cranky?

The sorry truth of it is we're all still tossing and turning in our bed-in-a-box mattress or wide awake on the red-eye, asking the same questions that have perplexed philosophers, prophets, poets, artists, alchemists, saints, mathematicians, and mystics for millenniums: *Why? What's the rest of it? Is this all there is? How do I get myself back on track? What am I supposed to be doing with my life? Is it too late for me to start over?*

All these questions are part of the human experience. All these questions deserve the respect of deep, reflective time-outs. For what enables this ancient and deeply personal search are those rare moments spent pondering our vast possibilities, which can't happen unless we acknowledge what we already have.

And when we do that, something almost magical happens. We begin to recognize that our lives actually are overflowing with gifts. The small moments of peace within the drama, the warm sweater on a cold day, the stranger's sudden smile, the glimpses of relief in hard times, a beloved child's hand in yours. How can we not be overwhelmed with gratitude at times like those?

Gratitude pulls back the scrim of the superficial and asks us to pause and consider what truly matters in our lives.

Once we understand that abundance and lack are also parallel stories and that each day we choose—consciously or unconsciously—which story we will tell ourselves today, a deep inner shift in our understanding occurs. Almost immediately our breathing slows down, our resting pulse isn't sprinting, and our souls find repose. Sometimes we call it "catching our breath" or the "Aha" moment. I call it a Well-Spent Moment, an unplugged pause so that another piece in our puzzlement can find its place. Once again, we experience a sense of wonder. No longer do we see the world as it is. Instead, we view the world as we are.

Yes, that old cliché about seeing the world through rose-colored glasses isn't such a bad idea—in fact, I have several pairs. When my day has gone haywire, it's time to put them on and reach for my Gratitude Journal. Just a few focused moments can redeem the rest of the day and the night. What always cheers and calms me is how simple, small, and often overlooked my daily gratitudes are. We discover the sacred in the ordinary, and we realize that every day is literally a gift. How we conduct our daily round, how we celebrate it, and how we cherish it is how we express our thankfulness to the Giver of all good. But a thank-you note is always appreciated.

The Ordinary Instant

Life changes fast.
Life changes in the instant.
You sit down to dinner and life as you know it ends.

—Joan Didion

But let's be real. Every day and night, bad things happen to good people. Suddenly and inexplicably, more often than anyone ever suspects, life stuns us with loss. A phone call in the middle of the night, a news bulletin across a screen, a pounding at the door. We lose a loved one or our job. We lose our home or our health. We lose our marriage or our life's savings. Without warning, hearts are broken, dreams are dashed, fortunes reversed, reputations tarnished. What was only a moment ago—and what we took for granted: serenity, sanity, security, safety, sameness—is ruthlessly snatched away, blown to smithereens, engulfed by a wave or burned to the ground. And we are left helplessly behind—bewildered, bereft, and incredulous—staring at the unimaginable now facing us.

Gone are the assumptions that sustained us, the expectations that shaped us, the illusions that propped us up. We feel as if life is over, and we are right. Life as we knew it is over. In an instant. An ordinary instant.

There are simply no words to express, or to console or encourage. There's no explanation, no reasoning, no self-help mantra, no belief big enough to surmount the anguish we feel at this moment. There's no secret on earth to help you come to grips with the vast unknown.

And yet, Gratitude can hold us together even as we're falling apart. It baffles me that this is true, and I wish that I didn't have firsthand understanding of this, but I do. Ironically, Gratitude's most powerful mysteries are often revealed when we are struggling during deep personal turmoil and overcome with doubt. Gratitude fills in the gaps. When we stumble in the darkness, rage in anger at the unfairness, and throw faith across the room. When we abandon all hope and cry ourselves to sleep, Gratitude waits patiently at the end of our bed to console and reassure us that we will get through whatever it is. And if we can't get over it, Gratitude reassures us that we will, eventually, get through what we can't get over, for there is a landscape larger than the one we can see now through our tears.

It's easy to be grateful when life hums—when there's money in the bank, you've got a marvelous job, the romance is exciting, or your marriage is in one of its sweet phases and you're healthy. But when you don't know how the bills will get paid, or you're not loved back, when you're reeling from a devastating diagnosis or your mortgage-free "forever" house has been swept down the street in a "no flood insurance" zone, "Thank you" isn't the phrase that immediately comes to mind.

It's hard to feel grateful when our hearts are broken and our dreams are dashed. However, it has been my experience that it doesn't really matter how we *feel*; what matters is that we *do* it. The Bible instructs us "to give thanks in all circumstances," but it doesn't tell us we have to be smiling while we say it. In Catholic and Eastern Orthodox faiths, tears have always been considered one of the special gifts of the Holy Spirit. The Talmud teaches that "even when the gates of Heaven are closed to prayers, they are open to tears," and in the Hebrew Old Testament, an entire book of the Bible is devoted to crying. It's called the Book of Lamentations. As the psalmist (56:8) recalls, "You keep track of all my sorrows. You have collected all my tears in your bottle. You have recorded each one in your book."

What book might that be?

Could it be a Divine Gratitude Journal?

I think so.

Once, during several seasons of devastating loss, I forced out a sarcastic litany of "thanks" because I knew it was the only way that I could mourn and move on (the downside of spiritual law that no one ever talks about is the unfortunate truth that once you understand a lesson, you can't play dumb). "There. I've thanked you for my misery and pain. Are you happy now? But don't you dare come near me," I cried, holding up my hand to Spirit in defiance, pushing away the very Love I needed most. "So, thanks a million. Now you go your way, and I'll go mine."

Naked, complete, bitter surrender. But only because I'd been overcome by sorrow. Almost immediately after that prayer, though, I was enfolded in a surreal sense of peace. To this day I don't understand the source of power, wisdom, strength, and love far greater than my own that carried me gently from my own private battlefield. Very soon after, the trajectory of my life was forever altered in miraculous ways. Spirit doesn't keep score and Gratitude doesn't keep count, other than to lift us up off the mat before Life's referee calls us out. This is how I've learned about Gratitude: *First the gesture, then the grace.*

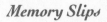

Memory Slips

Thankfulness is the beginning of gratitude. Gratitude is the completion of thankfulness. Thankfulness may consist merely of words. Gratitude is shown in acts.

—Henri Frederic Amiel

I've been writing about Gratitude for twenty-five years, both professionally and publicly (in my books) and privately (in my own Gratitude Journals). But back in 1991 when I first started experimenting with Gratitude as a spiritual catalyst for changing my life (in case you're wondering, skeptics make the best seekers), I recall being disappointed at how little I could find written on the subject, with the exception of a slender meditation by the Benedictine brother David Steindl-Rast titled *Gratefulness, the Heart of Prayer.* Certainly, there was no such thing as the Gratitude Journal, which was born because gratitude was such a new and amazing step toward changing how I perceived my life. I didn't want to forget how good Life was in the little moments.

Now when I type the word *Gratitude* into search engines today, the computer directs me to 154,000,000 books, quotes, websites, articles, newspapers, research projects, and products, and the number increases daily.

Among my favorites is the weighty tome *The Psychology of Gratitude*, edited by Robert A. Emmons and Michael E. McCullough, which is the first compilation of the empirical, scientific research on gratitude conducted by prominent scientists. When explaining how they chose their topic, they stated the following in the article "Counting Blessings versus Burdens: An Experimental Investigation of Gratitude and Subjective Well-Being in Daily Life":

> The construct of gratitude has inspired considerable interest in the general public...Although intuitively compelling, many of the general claims in popular books concerning the power of a grateful lifestyle are speculative and as yet scientifically untested. In one popular book on gratitude, for instance, the author asserts that "Whatever we are waiting for—peace of mind, contentment, grace...it will surely come to us, but only when we are ready to receive it with an open and grateful heart." (Breathnach, 1996)

Isn't this amazing? Although scientists are usually latecomers to the party, once they're with you, they're true believers. Through conducting highly focused and controlled studies on the nature of gratitude, its causes and consequences, Emmons and McCullough have concluded that people who keep Gratitude Journals are more optimistic than people who don't, take better care of themselves, exercise more regularly, report fewer physical ailments, and experience more alertness, enthusiasm, determination, and confidence to meet life's challenges; they also reported more moments of contentment than distress.

We know all this. But have we remembered it? If you're new to *Simple Abundance*, then whether you're aware of it or not, you've been hearing about gratitude and the Gratitude Journal for years. In fact, it's become so ubiquitous within the American conversation that it's almost the pop cultural, psychobabble equivalent of elevator music.

I wanted to address and acknowledge this directly before you embark on the *Simple Abundance* path to your authenticity. You may think you know about the power of Gratitude, but until you experience the miracle of Gratitude personally, you can't.

The Glad Game

I would maintain that thanks are the highest form of thought and that gratitude is happiness doubled by wonder.

—Gilbert K. Chesterton

A book that I adore is *Pollyanna in Hollywood* (1931) by Elizabeth Borton, one of several "Glad Book" authors in the fourteen-book series originally created by Eleanor H. Porter in 1913. The very title makes me smile, because the idea of playing Pollyanna's Glad Game in early Hollywood just as "the talkies" were introduced seems such delicious irony and a romp. But gratitude works anytime and everywhere. As the inscription in my book from a loving mother to her daughter leaving home to find her fame and fortune in the movies, reminds me today: "Always remember there's a reason to be glad, and an unexpected gift arrives when we're grateful."

Readers who have been with me before know that as far as I'm concerned Gratitude is fundamental to making it through the day. On the *Simple Abundance* path, Gratitude is not an option, and keeping a Gratitude Journal is the most important part of our daily ritual. When Gratitude becomes your spiritual practice, you discover that at the heart of *Simple Abundance* is the knowledge that you already possess all you need to be genuinely happy (and soon you might even become aware of how much you have). In twenty-five years, I have never once been let down by the grace of Gratitude, especially when the last thing I wanted to do was say, "Thank you." Gratitude is miraculous—and please, do quote me on that.

This is why I wanted to create a new special journal—a combination love letter and ledger of Life's largesse—so that we might encounter Gratitude in fresh ways.

Some days filling your Gratitude Journal will be easy. Other days the only thing you might be thankful for is that the day is over. That's okay—all loving relationships experience rough patches, which is why I've included a list of over one hundred often overlooked blessings to inspire you to search for the minor as well as the major chords of contentment. If you give thanks for five gifts every day, in two months you won't look at your life in the same way you do now. Gratitude can lead you, as it did me, away from the darkness of complicated need into the light of *Simple Abundance*.

I have often wondered what would have happened if, after the Fall, Adam and Eve returned to Eden's gate just to say, "Thank You. We blew it because we wanted it all and didn't appreciate how much we already had been given. Our idyll was brief, but our rapture knew no bounds. We were so blessed. Thank you, thank you, thank you. We'll carry and cherish these precious memories of exquisite pleasure and bliss within our souls throughout all eternity."

Do you think they would have been let back into Paradise?

I do.

Because every time we remember to say, "Thank you," we experience nothing less than Heaven on earth.

Dearest love and more gratitude
than words can say,

Sarah Ban Breathnach

July 2019

150 Often Overlooked Blessings

Faith. Faith in a Spirit possessing greater strength, wisdom, power, and love than you do. Faith in the ultimate goodness of Life. Faith in yourself. Faith that as you seek, you will find.

The dream that will not die, because you were born to love it into full being.

Answered prayers.

The kindness of strangers.

The warmth and security of home. Crossing the threshold and closing the door after a hard day.

Expressions of unconditional love and support.

Your health. The health of those you love.

That moment of relief when you realize that the pain has subsided.

A job that provides steady income while you pursue your dreams.

Feeling the presence of Spirit in your life.

Sinking into a warm, softly scented bath after a stressful day.

The aroma of something delicious wafting from the kitchen.

Not having to cook tonight.

Your boundless imagination.

When hope is restored.

Following your intuition and being delighted that you did.

Daydreams. Reveries. Textured, Technicolor nightscapes of happiness and good fortune that have you awakening with a smile.

Twelve hours of uninterrupted sleep.

Breakfast in bed.

Serenity as you pay bills.

Acceptance after struggle.

Seeing him or her and having your heart skip a beat.

Seeing him or her and finally feeling nothing.

Completely and utterly surrendering to *what is* and then waiting expectantly for the good that is to come.

An afternoon to do as you please.

Doing a great job and having it and your efforts appreciated.

Holding your child in your arms.

Delighting in other people's children.

Witnessing the birth of new life.

The times when your ideas "clicked" with others.

The fragrance of a vacation day.

The beach. The feel of the sand beneath your feet, the salty breeze, the warming rays of the sun.

A walk in the woods and becoming aware of life all around you.

Trying something new and loving it.

The desire for knowledge.

Two hours in a wonderful bookstore.

Waking up early enough to watch the sunrise with a cup of tea or coffee.

Watching the sunset.

Meeting a kindred spirit.

Meeting your soul mate(s) and recognizing that you have known each other before.

The moment when the veil is lifted from your eyes and you know that you know.

Hearing a piece of music that instantly touches your soul.

Being able to add that music to your collection immediately.

Reading a passage in a book or a poem that expresses exactly how you feel.

Memorizing a beautiful piece of poetry and sharing it with another in conversation.

Holding hands.

Having a congenial conversation with a stranger on a plane, train, or bus.

Successfully hailing a cab during rush hour.

A nap.

Realizing that there are no coincidences.

Nailing the punch line in a favorite joke. Hearing their laughter.

Relishing a wonderful movie. Liking it so much you want to see it again as the credits roll. Seeing it again.

Laughing so hard you can't catch your breath and your sides ache.

The sacred release of a good cry.

Bringing joy, happiness, and comfort to another person or creature.

The loyal, loving companionship of pets.

Feeling you're part of a loving and supportive community or church.

Finding a parking space exactly when you need one.

Summoning up the courage to surmount a challenge.

Taking tiny and big risks and having them pay off.

Investing time, creative energy, and emotion in yourself, then reaping the rich harvest of authentic success sown by Love.

Coming in after being caught in a soaking thunderstorm, getting out of wet clothes, and becoming warm and dry.

Meeting a deadline.

Making it to the game just in time to see her hit her first home run.

Friendship that endures and thrives despite the obstacles of time and distance.

Being able to trust another human being.

The experience of a pleasant déjà vu. The moment you realize it doesn't have to be déjà vu all over again unless you want it to.

Wisdom gleaned through life experiences (both yours and others'). Knowing how to use it.

Speaking another language.

Reading a book that changes your life.

Receiving flowers.

Moving on.

Letting go gracefully without regrets.

The first morsel of your favorite comfort food.

Savoring the scents of life (flowers, food, your lover, the earth, your child's hair).

The fresh feeling that immediately comes after a shower and washing your hair.

Being able to travel; the adventure of new places.

Room service.

The support and loving presence of sisters and/or brothers.

Achieving a long-sought-after goal. The moment when your accomplishment emotionally registers.

Feeling a sense of pride in yourself.

Wishing upon a star. Having your wish come true.

Finding your perfect scent.

Making eye contact and smiling with a gorgeous stranger.

A dance partner who makes you feel like Ginger Rogers (or Fred Astaire).

That person who takes your breath away when you are near or feel him or her next to you.

The first kiss.

Being with a person with whom you can communicate without words.

The moment you realize you'd marry your spouse all over again.

Sharing the holidays with people you really want to be with.

Easily switching car pool days.

Finding, having, and wearing something that makes you feel special.

Saying no to the bake sale without guilt.

A miracle.

Bargains at thrift shops, flea markets, garage sales.

The sense of relief throwing stuff out brings.

Your mentor.

The individual who inspired your career and made you believe that there is nothing as real as a dream.

The person who believed in you when you weren't able to believe in yourself.

A fortune cookie with just the right message.

The precious lingering memory of your mother's sweet scent. The comforting memory of your father's hand.

Being able to provide for the needs and wants of your loved ones.

The moment you are able to distinguish between your needs and your wants.

Watching others enjoy your creations, whether they are a meal, flowers from your garden, or a pair of pants you just ironed.

Being able to make clear, conscious, creative choices.

Air-conditioning on an excruciatingly hot and humid day.

Being upgraded to first class.

The contentment of sitting before a roaring fire on a winter's evening.

Receiving a love letter. Writing one.

All of the tragedy you and yours have escaped.

Becoming fascinated in a subject and learning more about it.

Hearing the words *I love you*.

The awareness of innocence.

The long-awaited phone call with good news.

When the repair bill is less than you'd expected.

A sense of humor during good and rough patches.

Not losing your temper.

Giving and receiving forgiveness after a painful estrangement.

Perfect timing.

Fitting into last year's clothes.

Knowing a favorite book awaits you at the end of a day.

Sleeping on the perfect pillow. The contentment of being wrapped in a favorite blanket, quilt, or goose-down comforter.

Sharing your aspirations for the future with a close friend.

Reawakening an old passion; discovering a new one.

The haven of a comforting shoulder to cry on; the warming embrace of a loved one.

Pampering yourself.

Listening to the whispers of your Authentic Self and taking her or his advice.

The generosity and hospitality of good neighbors.

Family and friends who remember funny or uplifting stories about your past that you've forgotten and share them with you.

Finding a lost pet.

Rediscovering old family photos.

Playing hooky.

The intimate bond of friendship that protects, nurtures, inspires, and comforts.

The man or woman in your life who is neither a past nor present love but simply a precious friend who adores you.

Waking up to a perfectly beautiful day for a planned outdoor event.

Working with people you enjoy being around. Working with people who are pleasant, kind, funny, considerate, and who honor your contribution.

An opportunity to interview for the dream job. Getting it.

Receiving the *perfect* gift. Finding one for someone else.

Catching a glimpse of yourself in the mirror and delighting in what you see.

Having your child appreciate your sense of humor.

An unexpected compliment that makes your day.

Enjoying the company of smart, witty, savvy people; delighting in stimulating conversation and holding your own.

Completing the crossword puzzle without help.

Looking fabulous at your class reunion.

Listening to the oldies and recalling happy moments.

A rare, relaxing break with your coworker during a hectic day.

Paying off your credit card balance.

Coming up with the perfect retort at the moment you need it and not two hours later.

The sound of raindrops on your roof at night.

Friends and family who can both truly rejoice with you and console in times of sorrow.

January

Time is the New Year's bountiful blessing: three hundred sixty-five bright mornings and starlit evenings; fifty-two promising weeks; twelve transformative months full of beautiful possibilities; and four splendid seasons. A simply abundant year to be savored with gratitude.

Gratitude unlocks the fullness of life. It turns what we have into enough, and more. It turns denial into acceptance, chaos to order, confusion to clarity. It can turn a meal into a feast, a house into a home, a stranger into a friend. Gratitude makes sense of our past, brings peace for today, and creates a vision for tomorrow.

—Melody Beattie

January 1

January 2

January 3

January 4

January 5

January 6

January 7

January 8

_____

January 9

_____

January 10

_____

January 11

_____

Gratitude helps you to grow and expand; gratitude brings joy and laughter into your life and into the lives of all those around you.

—Eileen Caddy

January 12

January 13

January 14

Just to be is a blessing. Just to live is holy.

—Rabbi Abraham Heschel

January 15

January 16

January 17

January 18

January 19

January 20

January 21

January 22

January 23

January 24

January 25

Gratitude is our most direct line to God and the angels. If we take the time, no matter how crazy and troubled we feel, we can find something to be thankful for. The more we seek gratitude, the more reason the angels will give us for gratitude and joy to exist in our lives.

—Terry Lynn Taylor

January 26

January 27

January 28

---

*Let's choose today to quench our thirst for the "good life" we
think others lead by acknowledging the good that already exists
in our own lives. We can then offer the Universe the gift of our
grateful hearts.*

—S.B.B.

January 29

_____

_____

_____

_____

January 30

_____

_____

_____

_____

January 31

_____

_____

_____

_____

_____

February

Take a real risk this month: Discover what makes you happy. Give thanks for the pleasures and pursuits you love. It will jump-start a glorious transformation. Begin to think of your life as a work in progress. Works in progress are never perfect. But changes can be made to the rough draft during rewrites. The beautiful, authentic life you are creating for yourself and those you love is your art.

Love wholeheartedly, be surprised, give thanks and praise—
then you will discover the fullness of your life.

—Brother David Steindl-Rast

February 1

February 2

February 3

February 4

February 5

February 6

February 7

February 8

February 9

February 10

February 11

Be thankful for what you have; you'll end up having more. If you concentrate on what you don't have, you will never, ever have enough.

—Oprah Winfrey

February 12

February 13

February 14

There is a calmness to a life lived in Gratitude, a quiet joy.
—Ralph H. Blum

February 15

_____
_____
_____
_____
_____

February 16

_____
_____
_____
_____
_____

February 17

_____
_____
_____
_____
_____

February 18

_____

_____

_____

_____

_____

February 19

_____

_____

_____

_____

_____

February 20

_____

_____

_____

_____

_____

February 21

_____

_____

_____

_____

_____

February 22

_____
_____
_____
_____

February 23

_____
_____
_____
_____

February 24

_____
_____
_____
_____

February 25

_____
_____
_____
_____

God has two dwellings, one in heaven, and the other in a meek and thankful heart.

—Izaak Walton

February 26

February 27

February 28

Grace is available for each of us every day—our spiritual daily bread—but we've got to remember to ask for it with a grateful heart and not worry about whether there will be enough for tomorrow.

—S.B.B.

February 29

_____

_____

_____

_____

_____

March

The *Simple Abundance* path is creative and practical as well as spiritual. If you consciously work to bring more Gratitude, Simplicity, Order, Harmony, and Beauty into your daily round, your world will be transformed, and you will discover the Joy of knowing your personal pattern of authentic pleasures and preferences.

Feeling grateful or appreciative of someone or something in your life actually attracts more of the things that you appreciate and value into your life. And, the more of your life that you like and appreciate, the healthier you'll be. Science is now documenting what women have known intuitively for millennia: that "thinking with your heart" will lead you in the right direction.

—Christiane Northrup, MD

March 1

March 2

March 3

March 4

March 5

March 6

March 7

March 8

_____

_____

_____

_____

_____

March 9

_____

_____

_____

_____

_____

March 10

_____

_____

_____

_____

_____

March 11

_____

_____

_____

_____

_____

The first wealth is health.

—Ralph Waldo Emerson

March 12

March 13

March 14

"Thank you" is the best prayer that anyone could say. I say that one a lot. "Thank you" expresses extreme gratitude, humility, understanding.

—Alice Walker

March 15

_____

_____

_____

_____

_____

March 16

_____

_____

_____

_____

_____

March 17

_____

_____

_____

_____

_____

March 18

_____
_____
_____
_____
_____

March 19

_____
_____
_____
_____
_____

March 20

_____
_____
_____
_____
_____

March 21

_____
_____
_____
_____
_____

March 22

March 23

March 24

March 25

One can never pay in gratitude; one can only pay "in kind" somewhere else in life.

—Anne Morrow Lindbergh

March 26

_____

_____

_____

_____

_____

March 27

_____

_____

_____

_____

_____

March 28

_____

_____

_____

_____

_____

True gratitude comes even before the events to which it is related.
The gratitude came first, the healing followed.

— *The Christian Science Monitor*

March 29

March 30

March 31

April

At the heart of *Simple Abundance* is an authentic awakening, one that resonates with your soul: You already possess all you need to be genuinely happy right now. Today. All you truly need is an awareness of the abundance that is already yours. Gratitude jumpstarts this spiritual wonder. Let your heart bask in the transforming power of gratefulness.

Enjoy the little things, for one day you may look back and realize they were the big things.

—Robert Brault

April 1

April 2

April 3

April 4

_____

_____

_____

_____

_____

April 5

_____

_____

_____

_____

_____

April 6

_____

_____

_____

_____

_____

April 7

_____

_____

_____

_____

_____

April 8

_____

_____

_____

_____

April 9

_____

_____

_____

_____

April 10

_____

_____

_____

_____

April 11

_____

_____

_____

_____

When I started counting my blessings, my whole life turned around.

—Willie Nelson

April 12

April 13

April 14

None is more impoverished than the one who has no gratitude. Gratitude is a currency that we can mint for ourselves and spend without fear of bankruptcy.

—Fred De Witt Van Amburgh

April 15

April 16

April 17

April 18

_____
_____
_____
_____
_____

April 19

_____
_____
_____
_____
_____

April 20

_____
_____
_____
_____
_____

April 21

_____
_____
_____
_____
_____

April 22

April 23

April 24

April 25

Silent gratitude isn't very much use to anyone.

—Gertrude Stein

April 26

_____
_____
_____
_____
_____

April 27

_____
_____
_____
_____
_____

April 28

_____
_____
_____
_____
_____

*Optimism may keep you happy, but gratitude keeps everything—
especially your losses—in perspective.*

—Koa Beck

April 29

_____

_____

_____

_____

_____

April 30

_____

_____

_____

_____

_____

May

Simple Abundance is a daily meditation on the boundless treasure and spiritual replenishment of a perfect solitary hour. Search for a new sacred space out in the world: a shady grove of trees in an old cemetery; a beautiful public garden that's new to you; a museum gallery, the stacks of an old library, the hush of a quiet chapel, even an outdoor café. Each day offers you the gifts of Well-Spent Moments patiently waiting for your pleasure.

Be grateful for the home you have, knowing that at this moment, all you have is all you need.

—S.B.B.

May 1

May 2

May 3

May 4

May 5

May 6

May 7

May 8

May 9

May 10

May 11

Walk through the different rooms where you eat, sleep, and live. Bless the walls, the roof, the windows and the foundation. Give thanks for your home exactly as it exists today: sift and sort, simplify, and bring order to the home you have. Realize that the home of your dreams dwells within.

—S.B.B.

May 12

May 13

May 14

Every spirit builds itself a house, and beyond its house a world, and beyond its world a heaven. Know then that world exists for you.

—Ralph Waldo Emerson

May 15

May 16

May 17

May 18

_____

_____

_____

_____

May 19

_____

_____

_____

_____

May 20

_____

_____

_____

_____

May 21

_____

_____

_____

_____

May 22

_____
_____
_____
_____
_____

May 23

_____
_____
_____
_____
_____

May 24

_____
_____
_____
_____
_____

May 25

_____
_____
_____
_____
_____

The ordinary acts we practice every day at home are of more importance to the soul than their simplicity might suggest.

—Thomas Moore

May 26

May 27

May 28

We shape our dwellings, and afterwards our dwellings shape us.
—Winston Churchill

May 29

May 30

May 31

June

When we embrace our creative impulses, we live our truth even if what we think we're doing is just planting a flower bed, cooking a meal, nurturing a child, editing a book, producing a television show, sewing a hem, writing a brief, teaching a craft, composing a song, closing a deal, safely guarding children across the street. For an Artist of the Everyday, each small, loving task is a brushstroke on the canvas of our lives.

Meanings, moods, the whole scale of our inner experience, finds in nature the "correspondences" through which we may know our boundless selves.

—Kathleen Raine

June 1

June 2

June 3

June 4

June 5

June 6

June 7

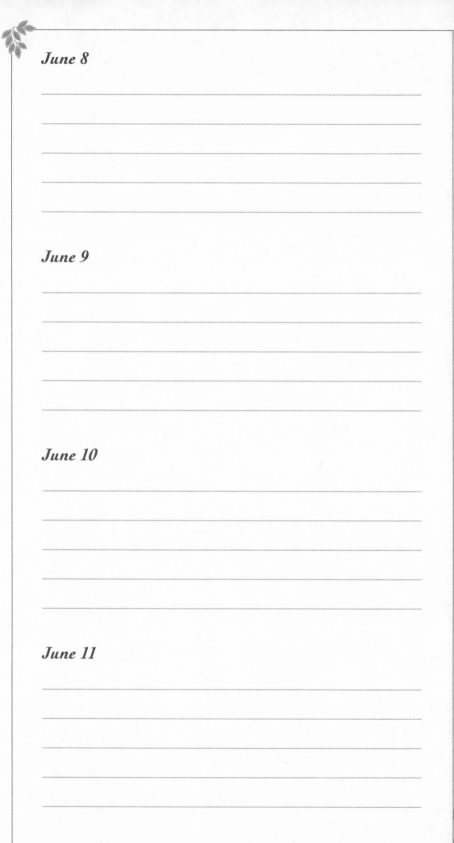

June 8

June 9

June 10

June 11

We learn each day how cultivating gratitude tills the soil of our souls, and then how the seeds of simplicity, order, harmony, beauty, and joy send their roots deep down into the earth of everyday existence.

—S.B.B.

June 12

_____

_____

_____

_____

_____

June 13

_____

_____

_____

_____

_____

June 14

_____

_____

_____

_____

_____

Within your heart, keep one still, secret spot where dreams may go.

—Louise Driscoll

June 15

June 16

June 17

June 18

June 19

June 20

June 21

June 22

June 23

June 24

June 25

Both abundance and lack exist simultaneously in our lives, as parallel realities. It is always our conscious choice which secret garden we will tend . . . when we choose not to focus on what is missing from our lives but are grateful for the abundance that's present—love, health, family, friends, work, the joys of nature and personal pursuits that bring us pleasure—the wasteland of illusion falls away and we experience Heaven on earth.

—S.B.B.

June 26

June 27

June 28

At times, our own light goes out and is rekindled by a spark from another person. Each of us has cause to think with deep gratitude of those who have lighted the flame within us.

—Albert Schweitzer

June 29

_____

_____

_____

_____

_____

June 30

_____

_____

_____

_____

_____

July

July is generous with her authentic gifts. Once again, the days are sunny and hot. Joyful simplicities invite us to discover a frosty glass of lemonade, ripe strawberries and cream, an afternoon swim, or a nap in a hammock. Our smiles deepen, our laughter increases, our hearts become more open. Everyday epiphanies encourage us to cherish everything, especially the small choices close to home.

When we recall the past, we usually find that it is the simplest things—not the great occasions—that in retrospect give off the greatest glow of happiness.

—Bob Hope

July 1

July 2

July 3

July 4

_____
_____
_____
_____
_____

July 5

_____
_____
_____
_____
_____

July 6

_____
_____
_____
_____
_____

July 7

_____
_____
_____
_____
_____

July 8

July 9

July 10

July 11

Work and live to serve others, to leave the world a little better than you found it and garner for yourself as much peace of mind as you can. This is happiness.

—David Sarnoff

July 12

_____

_____

_____

_____

_____

July 13

_____

_____

_____

_____

_____

July 14

_____

_____

_____

_____

_____

The three grand essentials to happiness in life are something to do, something to love, and something to hope for.

—Joseph Addison

July 15

_____

_____

_____

_____

_____

July 16

_____

_____

_____

_____

_____

July 17

_____

_____

_____

_____

_____

July 18

July 19

July 20

July 21

July 22

_____
_____
_____
_____
_____

July 23

_____
_____
_____
_____
_____

July 24

_____
_____
_____
_____
_____

July 25

_____
_____
_____
_____
_____

There is no duty we so much underrate as the duty of being happy. By being happy we sow anonymous benefits upon the world.

—Robert Louis Stevenson

July 26

July 27

July 28

Happiness is not a possession to be prized. It is a quality of thought, a state of mind.

—Daphne du Maurier

July 29

July 30

July 31

August

This August treat yourself to the passionate pursuit of pleasure. Rediscovering, recovering, and celebrating your creativity—the sacred conduit to your Authentic Self—is the perfect private getaway. It is never too late to reclaim your individual gifts, resuscitate a dream, or finally honor your intuition and take a new path.

I awoke this morning with devout thanksgiving for my friends, the old and the new.

—Ralph Waldo Emerson

August 1

August 2

August 3

August 4

August 5

August 6

August 7

August 8

August 9

August 10

August 11

Each friend represents a world in us, a world possibly not born until they arrive, and it is only by this meeting that a new world is born.

—Anaïs Nin

August 12

_____
_____
_____
_____
_____

August 13

_____
_____
_____
_____
_____

August 14

_____
_____
_____
_____
_____

Friendships begin with liking or gratitude.

—George Eliot

August 15

_____
_____
_____
_____
_____

August 16

_____
_____
_____
_____
_____

August 17

_____
_____
_____
_____
_____

August 18

August 19

August 20

August 21

August 22

_____
_____
_____
_____
_____

August 23

_____
_____
_____
_____
_____

August 24

_____
_____
_____
_____
_____

August 25

_____
_____
_____
_____
_____

Be grateful for the gifts of sharing your earthly span with creatures who comfort. Animals are our spiritual companions, living proof of a simply abundant source of love. None of us feel alone. And if there is a gift, then surely, there must be a Giver.

—S.B.B.

August 26

_____
_____
_____
_____
_____

August 27

_____
_____
_____
_____
_____

August 28

_____
_____
_____
_____
_____

Your friend is . . . your field which you sow with love and reap with thanksgiving.

—Kahlil Gibran

August 29

August 30

August 31

September

Authentic success is not about accumulating but letting go, because all you have is all you truly need. Authentic success is feeling good about who you are, appreciating where you've been, celebrating your achievements, and honoring the distance you've already come. If you're starting a new adventure, blessings on your courage.

To love what you do and feel that it matters—how could anything be more fun?

—Katharine Graham

September 1

_____

_____

_____

_____

_____

September 2

_____

_____

_____

_____

_____

September 3

_____

_____

_____

_____

_____

September 4

_____
_____
_____
_____
_____

September 5

_____
_____
_____
_____
_____

September 6

_____
_____
_____
_____
_____

September 7

_____
_____
_____
_____
_____

September 8

September 9

September 10

September 11

Work is love made visible.

—Kahlil Gibran

September 12

_____
_____
_____
_____
_____

September 13

_____
_____
_____
_____
_____

September 14

_____
_____
_____
_____
_____

The pitcher cries for water to carry and a person for work that is Real.

—Marge Piercy

September 15

September 16

September 17

September 18

_____
_____
_____
_____
_____

September 19

_____
_____
_____
_____
_____

September 20

_____
_____
_____
_____
_____

September 21

_____
_____
_____
_____
_____

September 22

_____
_____
_____
_____
_____

September 23

_____
_____
_____
_____
_____

September 24

_____
_____
_____
_____
_____

September 25

_____
_____
_____
_____
_____

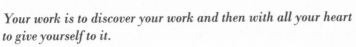

Your work is to discover your work and then with all your heart to give yourself to it.

—Buddha

September 26

_____
_____
_____
_____
_____

September 27

_____
_____
_____
_____
_____

September 28

_____
_____
_____
_____
_____

We are made for larger ends than Earth can encompass. Oh, let us be true to our exalted destiny.

—Catherine Booth

September 29

_____

_____

_____

_____

_____

September 30

_____

_____

_____

_____

_____

October

Study the cycles of Mother Nature, the garden whispers, for they correspond with the cycles of your soul's growth. Quiet your mind. Rope in the restlessness. Be here, wherever that might be. Learn to labor. Learn to wait in joyful anticipation. Give thanks for the harvest, and let that harvest be a simply abundant lifestyle rooted not in the world but in what matters most to you.

As we become curators of our own contentment on the Simple Abundance *path . . . we learn to savor the small with a grateful heart.*

—S.B.B.

October 1

October 2

October 3

October 4

October 5

October 6

October 7

October 8

October 9

October 10

October 11

Once we discover how to appreciate the timeless values in our daily experiences, we can enjoy the best things in life.

—Harry Hepner

October 12

_____
_____
_____
_____
_____

October 13

_____
_____
_____
_____
_____

October 14

_____
_____
_____
_____
_____

*It isn't the big pleasures that count the most; it's making a great
deal out of the little ones.*

—Jean Webster

October 15

October 16

October 17

October 18

_____
_____
_____
_____
_____

October 19

_____
_____
_____
_____
_____

October 20

_____
_____
_____
_____
_____

October 21

_____
_____
_____
_____
_____

October 22

_____

_____

_____

_____

_____

October 23

_____

_____

_____

_____

_____

October 24

_____

_____

_____

_____

_____

October 25

_____

_____

_____

_____

_____

To be really great in little things, to be truly noble and heroic in the insipid details of everyday life, is a virtue so rare as to be worthy of canonization.

—Harriet Beecher Stowe

October 26

_____
_____
_____
_____
_____

October 27

_____
_____
_____
_____
_____

October 28

_____
_____
_____
_____
_____

I am beginning to learn that it is the sweet, simple things of life which are the real ones after all.

—Laura Ingalls Wilder

October 29

_____
_____
_____
_____
_____

October 30

_____
_____
_____
_____
_____

October 31

_____
_____
_____
_____
_____

November

Offer grace for the bounty of goodness. Raise the song of harvest home, the glass of good cheer, the heart overflowing with joy. We have so much for which to be thankful. So much about which to smile, so much to share. So much, that in this season of plenty, we can embrace the season of relinquishment. For all we have is all we need.

Gratitude is the inward feeling of kindness received. Thankfulness is the natural impulse to express that feeling. Thanksgiving is the following of that impulse.

—Henry Van Dyke

November 1

November 2

November 3

November 4

November 5

November 6

November 7

November 8

November 9

November 10

November 11

Authentic success is being so grateful for the many blessings bestowed on you and yours that you can share your portion with others.

—S.B.B.

November 12

November 13

November 14

Let your thanksgiving for all that is rise above the din of disappointment—opportunities lost, mistakes made, the clamor of all that has not yet come.

—S.B.B.

November 15

November 16

November 17

November 18

_____
_____
_____
_____
_____

November 19

_____
_____
_____
_____
_____

November 20

_____
_____
_____
_____
_____

November 21

_____
_____
_____
_____
_____

November 22

_____

_____

_____

_____

_____

November 23

_____

_____

_____

_____

_____

November 24

_____

_____

_____

_____

_____

November 25

_____

_____

_____

_____

_____

I've had a remarkable life. I seem to be in such good places at the right time. You know, if you were to ask me to sum my life up in one word, gratitude.

—Dietrich Bonhoeffer

November 26

November 27

November 28

*Gratitude is not only the memory but the homage of the heart
rendered to God for his goodness.*

—N. P. Willis

November 29

_____
_____
_____
_____
_____

November 30

_____
_____
_____
_____
_____

December

December is all about gifts. Nothing but gifts... Gifts tied with heartstrings. Gifts that surprise and delight. Gifts that nurture the hearts of both the giver and the given. Perfect gifts. Authentic gifts. Unconditional Love. Selflessness. Trust. Faith. Forgiveness. Wholeness. Second chances. Comfort. Joy. Peace. Reassurance. Rejoicing. Generosity. Compassion. Charity. Wonder. Acceptance. Courage. To give such gifts! To truly open our hearts to gratefully receive such gifts.

One can never pay in gratitude; one can only pay in kind somewhere else in a life.

—Anne Morrow Lindbergh

December 1

_____

_____

_____

_____

_____

December 2

_____

_____

_____

_____

_____

December 3

_____

_____

_____

_____

_____

December 4

_____

_____

_____

_____

_____

December 5

_____

_____

_____

_____

_____

December 6

_____

_____

_____

_____

_____

December 7

_____

_____

_____

_____

_____

December 8

_____

_____

_____

_____

_____

December 9

_____

_____

_____

_____

_____

December 10

_____

_____

_____

_____

_____

December 11

_____

_____

_____

_____

_____

This is a wonderful day. I've never seen this one before.
—Maya Angelou

December 12

_____

_____

_____

_____

_____

December 13

_____

_____

_____

_____

_____

December 14

_____

_____

_____

_____

_____

There is only one real deprivation . . . and that is not to be able to give one's gifts to those one loves most.

—May Sarton

December 15

_____

_____

_____

_____

December 16

_____

_____

_____

_____

December 17

_____

_____

_____

_____

_____

December 18

_____

_____

_____

_____

_____

December 19

_____

_____

_____

_____

_____

December 20

_____

_____

_____

_____

_____

December 21

_____

_____

_____

_____

_____

December 22

_____

_____

_____

_____

_____

December 23

_____

_____

_____

_____

_____

December 24

_____

_____

_____

_____

_____

December 25

_____

_____

_____

_____

_____

God has given us two hands, one to receive with and the other to give with.

—Billy Graham

December 26

_____
_____
_____
_____
_____

December 27

_____
_____
_____
_____
_____

December 28

_____
_____
_____
_____
_____

Give thanks. Wait. Watch what happens. Get excited. Open your arms as wide as you can to receive all the miracles with your name on them. Godspeed.

—S.B.B.

December 29

_____

_____

_____

_____

_____

December 30

_____

_____

_____

_____

_____

December 31

_____

_____

_____

_____

_____

The Measure of Our Days

A Wealth of Well-Spent Moments

In the coming years we shall need all the charm, aplomb and philosophy we can get. It will be the task of women to keep the world from despond...

We will create beauty with whatever materials are at hand. We will fan the embers of kindness in a brute-stricken world... We will heal and hold to our hearts the wounded, the young, the needy. It is a great privilege to be a woman today.

—Margery Wilson

It's occurred to me that when we think about Gratitude, what we're really doing is meditating about happiness. The pursuit of happiness or the stumbling upon it; the recognition or the remembering of it; the acknowledgment and appreciation of those precious, fleeting moments make a difference in how we feel. When we discover what triggers smiles and sublime spiritual serendipity, we find the truest measure of our days.

One of my favorite ways of keeping Gratitude alive, especially during these turbulent times, is by noticing the Well-Spent Moments of each day.

What is a "Well-Spent Moment"? The expression is aspirational—we spend way too little time and attention on the things that give us genuine contentment. More to the point, though, the things that matter most are priceless. Those moments of connection, kindness, laughter, encouragement, and reassurance; flashes of intuition, inspiration, and personal coincidences occur all the time but are missed because we're busy worrying about the glass being half-empty.

In June 1942, six months after Pearl Harbor and during America's first summer at war, *Vogue* magazine took up the idea of "Well-Spent Moments." *Vogue* recognized the radical change that had taken place in the lives of its readers. "Whatever the change, whether we have a little or a lot of money; whether we have a little or a lot of time, we will want that money and that time to bring in the biggest returns." Theirs was a practical focus, and ours certainly can be that. But let's not forget the more transcendent, the more ephemeral moments, which are worthy of our time and attention too.

The end pages of your Gratitude Journal have been left blank, so it can act as a net for catching stray appreciations. Life's Well-Spent Moments hover in our awareness like floating bubbles. Try to capture and cherish every one.